My Islam Taught Me My Good Manners

TEACHING MANNERS TO MUSLIM KIDS FROM THE HOLY QURAN AND SUNNAH

BY THE SINCERE SEEKER KIDS COLLECTION

My Islam taught me to greet others with *Salam Alaykum* and to smile; it's Sunnah!

My Islam taught me to be good to others and treat everyone the way I want to be treated.

My Islam taught me to always be kind to animals.

My Islam taught me to always obey and help my parents.

My Islam taught me to forgive others and not hold grudges.

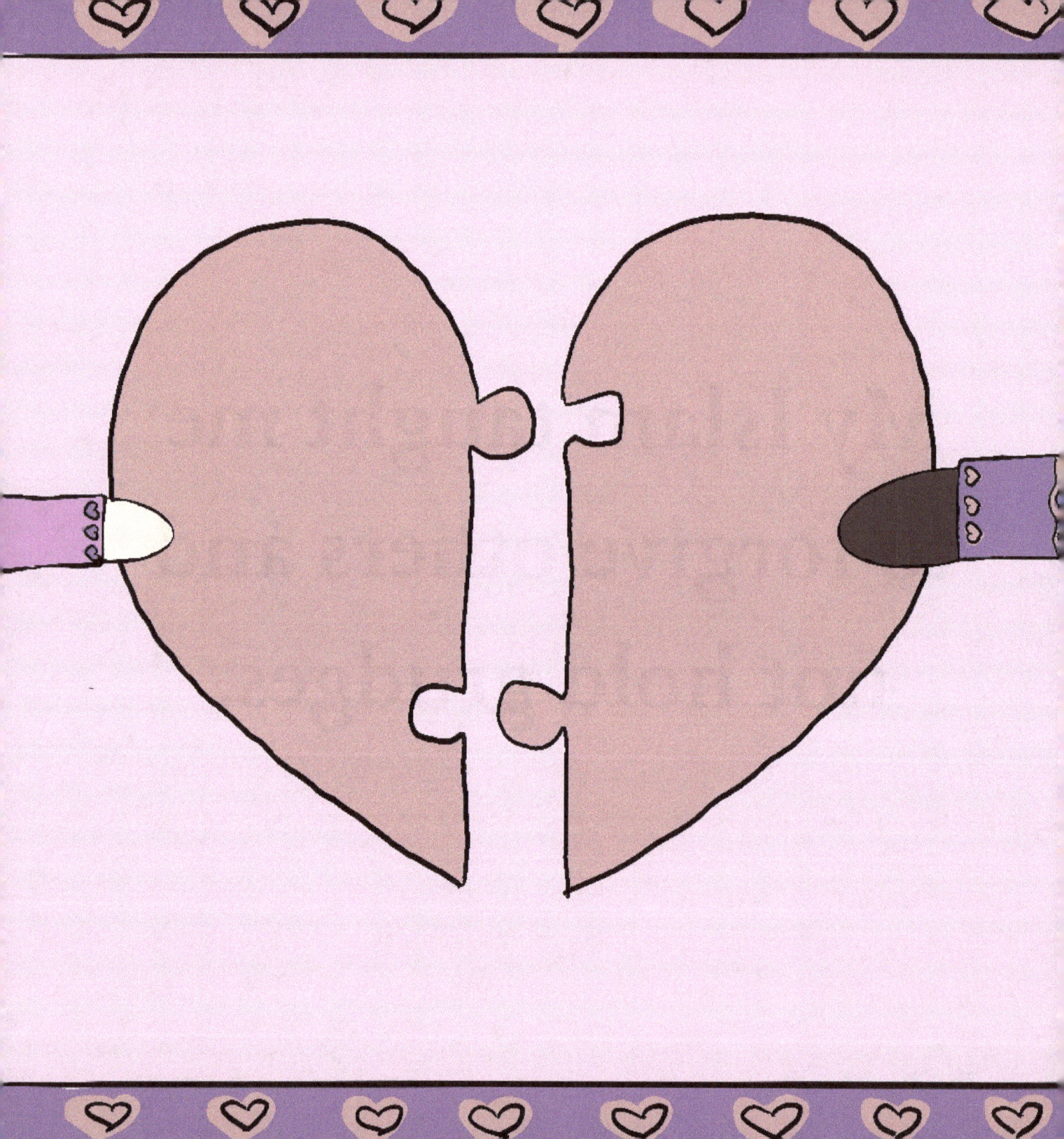

My Islam taught me not to hurt anyone.

My Islam taught me to be patient, not lose my cool and get angry!

My Islam taught me to say Bismillah before I eat and use my right hand.

My Islam taught me to say *Alhamdulillah* when I sneeze.

My Islam taught me to give to others, especially those in need.

My Islam taught me to speak kindly and use my indoor voice.

My Islam taught me to keep my promises and not break them.

MY MAMA MADE
PIZZA FOR US

My Islam taught me to honor my guests and offer them food and drinks!

My Islam taught me to always remember Allah, and He will remember me!

My Islam taught me never to cheat, whether on homework or when playing a board game with my family and friends.

My Islam taught me to always be honest and never lie.

My Islam taught me to always be grateful and thank Allah and those who help me.

My Islam taught me to clean myself after using the bathroom, clip my fingernails and toenails, brush my teeth and use a miswak.

My Islam taught me that my God, Allah, is One and only Him and that I should love Allah & obey Him!

My Islam taught me to share some of what I have with others because sharing is caring!

My Islam taught me to read the Holy Quran daily– it's Allah's Words! This helps me learn about Allah and gain knowledge!

SALAM

WA ALAYKUM ASALAM

CHARITY

My Islam taught me to follow the way of my Prophet Muhammad, peace be upon him. That's called following the Sunnah!

My Islam taught me to always pray my five daily prayers to Allah to live a successful life.

The End.

www.ingramcontent.com/pod-product-compliance
Lightning Source LLC
Chambersburg PA
CBHW081307140626
46546CB00022B/3448